Original title:
Beyond the Bars

Author: Swan Charm
ISBN HARDBACK: 978-9908-1-2335-6
ISBN PAPERBACK: 978-9908-1-2336-3
ISBN EBOOK: 978-9908-1-2337-0

The Sound of Open Air

Laughter dances, sweet and clear,
Voices mingled, joy draws near.
Colors burst in vibrant spry,
Where open hearts and spirits fly.

Breezes carry tales of cheer,
Fleeting moments, memories dear.
Underneath the sun's warm kiss,
Every heartbeat sings in bliss.

Embracing the Unfurling

Petals bloom in morning light,
Nature's canvas, pure delight.
Sparkling eyes and open arms,
Welcoming all the world's charms.

Drums are beating, feet take flight,
Dancing shadows in the night.
Whispers weave through azure skies,
As spirits soar, their laughter flies.

An Odyssey of the Mind

Wanderlust through tales untold,
Imagined lands of dreams unfold.
Boundless thoughts, like rivers flow,
In festive lands where hopes brightly glow.

Canvas bright with colors wide,
Story threads meet hearts that bide.
Every chapter, spark ignites,
Creating joy in starry nights.

Journeys Untold

Every path a whispered song,
Adventures waiting, free and strong.
Through the laughter, bonds are made,
In every step, no joy will fade.

Banners wave with colors bold,
Tales of kinship, warmth retold.
United voices rise and blend,
In this gathering, hearts transcend.

A World Awaits

Bright lights twinkle all around,
Laughter dances on the breeze.
Joyous hearts and smiles abound,
Together, we embrace the ease.

Colors burst in vibrant cheer,
Songs of love fill every space.
In this moment, hold it near,
In unity, we find our place.

Shadows of Release

Balloons rise towards the night,
Fleeting moments, pure delight.
Whispers dance in dusk's soft hue,
Celebration's sweet adieu.

Dreams unfurl like ribbons bright,
In the warmth, we share our light.
Lift your glass, let spirits soar,
In this joy, we seek for more.

The Unfurling Sky

Stars awaken, one by one,
Bathed in glow, the night has spun.
Underneath this vast embrace,
Hearts unite in a wondrous space.

Fireworks paint the heavens high,
Each burst a spark, a hopeful sigh.
We gather close, hand in hand,
In this spell, together we stand.

Wings of Resilience

Festive beats, the rhythm sways,
Feet that dance in lively bays.
With each step, let troubles fade,
Life's a joy, let's not invade.

Through the trials, we have grown,
With our laughter, seeds are sown.
Wings will carry us so high,
Together, we will touch the sky.

Boundless Horizons

Beneath the sun's bright gleam, we play,
With laughter spilling, joy leads the way.
A canvas of dreams in colors so bold,
Together in moments, our stories unfold.

The skies are painted with hues of delight,
As hearts rise like kites in the warm, gentle light.
With every embrace, the world feels alive,
In the dance of the festive, our spirits thrive.

Veils of Reality

Through gauzy curtains, magic appears,
Whispers of wonder, releasing our fears.
A festival of dreams that shimmer and sway,
As reality blends with the joy of the day.

With every soft giggle and spark of the night,
We celebrate moments that feel so right.
The veils of the mundane fall away with each cheer,
In this radiant space, we let go of our fear.

Dancing with Possibility

In the rhythm of laughter, our spirits ignite,
We twirl through the stars, oh, what a sight!
Each step a promise, each spin a chance,
As we embrace the world with a jubilant dance.

With eyes full of wonder and hearts open wide,
We chase the bright whispers, let magic be our guide.
Dancing through life, with hope intertwined,
In this festive realm, our dreams are aligned.

The Lattice of Hope

Woven together, threads of our dreams,
A tapestry bright, bursting at seams.
In the lattice of hope, we find our own way,
Each moment a treasure, each laugh here to stay.

Together we gather, uniting our grace,
In this festive spirit, we find our place.
With lights all aglow, we share our delight,
Building a world where our hearts take flight.

The Color of Distant Dreams

In twilight hues, bright spirits dance,
A laughter-filled night, a wistful glance.
Banners wave, in a gentle breeze,
As joy unfolds, hearts drift with ease.

Stars blink above, a playful show,
The world adorned with a vibrant glow.
Each song sung, a thread of light,
Binding us close, in the warm night.

Footsteps echo on cobblestone,
Where whispers of joy are softly sown.
A tapestry rich, woven in cheer,
Holding us tight, drawing us near.

With every toast, and every cheer,
We paint the night with dreams sincere.
In the color of love, we bask and beam,
Together we share the distant dream.

Reaching for the Invisible

Hands stretched wide toward the azure sky,
Where dreams reside, and hopes can fly.
Each twinkling star holds a secret wish,
We reach for more, with every swish.

A festival blooms, with laughter and glee,
In this carnival of love, we long to be free.
The pulse of the night, a vibrant song,
Echoes our hearts, where we all belong.

Invisible threads connect us all,
As colors swirl, in this grand hall.
Together we dance, a radiant spree,
In the heart of the night, just you and me.

With every step, we chase the light,
Filling the air, with sheer delight.
Reaching for dreams, so bold, and bright,
In the festive world, we take flight.

Dreams Unchained

In the festival's heart, where laughter rings,
We shed the weight of mundane things.
With open arms, and spirits high,
We dance with dreams, beneath the sky.

Fireflies flicker, like thoughts set free,
In the night's embrace, just you and me.
The rhythm of joy beats soft and low,
In every glance, our passions glow.

Balloons ascend, like hopes on a string,
Each burst of color, a challenge to cling.
Unchained from limits, we spiral and soar,
In this vivid dream, we seek for more.

With every cheer, and every song,
We celebrate where we truly belong.
Dreams unchained, and hearts ajar,
In this festive night, we reach for the stars.

The Silent Yearning

Beneath the bright lights, where silence breaks,
A yearning stirs, in the joy that wakes.
We gather close, in this festive wreath,
Sharing whispers, and tales beneath.

The clock strikes joy, as moments unfold,
In every heartbeat, stories untold.
The warmth of togetherness wraps us tight,
As twilight blooms into the night.

Each glance exchanged, a secret spark,
Illuminates feelings that glow in the dark.
In vibrant laughter, and soft refrain,
We gather strength, from the silent pain.

With every hug, and gentle cheer,
We find the courage, we seek so near.
In the dance of hearts, with spirits so bright,
We weave our hopes, in the festive light.

Echoes of Possibility

In the glow of the evening fair,
Laughter dances on the air.
Colors splash and spirits rise,
Underneath the endless skies.

Hope ignites with each new cheer,
Echoes linger, bright and clear.
Dreams unfold in joyous flight,
Casting shadows, pure delight.

A Glimpse Through the Grate

Glimmers sneak through rusty bars,
Whispers of the moon and stars.
Voices blend in mirthful song,
A festive flow that won't be long.

Joyful rhythms pulse and swell,
In this place where stories dwell.
Each moment a brush of fate,
Through the grates, we celebrate.

The Daring Leap

With hearts ablaze, we take the chance,
In time's embrace, we start to dance.
A daring leap, we soar so high,
Embracing dreams beneath the sky.

Hands entwined, as laughter swells,
While every pause a story tells.
In every grin, a bond so tight,
We leap together into light.

Flickering Flames of Will

A spark ignites in joyful hearts,
Flickering flames where hope imparts.
Each cheer a torch, a guiding star,
Together we shine, no matter how far.

The warmth of laughter fills the night,
As dreams awaken in the light.
Bound by love, we know the thrill,
We gather strength from flickering will.

The Fabric of Emancipation

Colors bright, weaving dreams anew,
Threads of hope in vibrant hue.
Joyous laughter fills the air,
As freedom dances everywhere.

Festive songs echo through the land,
Unites us all with a helping hand.
Together we rise, unbound and free,
A tapestry of unity we see.

Celebrating all that we've achieved,
With every moment, we believe.
In the heart of night, we sing and cheer,
The fabric of love, woven near.

With each stitch, a story shared,
Moments cherished, lives declared.
In a world that opens wide,
Freedom's joy, our vibrant guide.

Seizing the Light

Beneath the stars, our spirits soar,
Radiant hopes, we can't ignore.
With laughter bright, we greet the dawn,
In every heart, a new light drawn.

Celebration fills the endless sky,
As dreams take flight, we reach up high.
In the rhythm of joy, we sway,
Seizing the light, come what may.

With every heart, we share the glow,
Embracing moments, letting go.
Together we shine, a dazzling sight,
In this grand dance of pure delight.

The world around sparkles and beams,
As we embrace each other's dreams.
With open eyes, together we dare,
To seize the light, joy everywhere.

Whispers of Hope

In the heart of the night, we gather near,
Laughter like stars, bright and clear.
Candles flicker, dreams take flight,
Whispers of hope in the soft twilight.

Joy in our voices, a melody sweet,
Dancing together, our hearts skip a beat.
Colors of life, vibrant and bold,
Stories of warmth in the chill of the cold.

With every embrace, bonds intertwine,
Moments like this, truly divine.
Banners of joy flutter in the breeze,
Whispers of hope bring us to our knees.

The Bridge to Tomorrow

Across the river, a bridge of light,
Steps made of laughter, shining and bright.
We walk hand in hand, the future in sight,
A celebration of dreams, taking flight.

Fireworks burst in the twilight sky,
Colors explode, as wishes fly by.
A tapestry woven with threads of delight,
The bridge to tomorrow, a beautiful sight.

With each heartbeat, the rhythm of cheer,
Hope in our hearts, drawing us near.
Voices united, raising a song,
Together we'll journey, where we belong.

Flight of the Captive Mind

In the cages of thought, we dance and we spin,
Wings of imagination begin to begin.
Joyful thoughts like birds take to the sky,
Free from the shadows, we laugh and we fly.

Colors of freedom paint paths anew,
Every new vision brings laughter, a view.
The chains of the past vanish, unseen,
In the flight of the captive, we find what's serene.

Whispers of courage call out from the dark,
Together we soar, igniting the spark.
With hearts full of wonder, spirits so bright,
We paint the horizon, a beautiful sight.

Fragments of Liberation

In the radiance of joy, we break the mold,
Fragments of liberation, stories unfold.
Shattering silence, dancing in glee,
Moments like these set our spirits free.

Colors collide in a brilliant display,
Unity blooms in the brightest array.
With every step, we reclaim the night,
Fragments of liberation, our hearts unite.

Voices together, a powerful sound,
In the echoes of love, new wisdom is found.
Celebrate life, in all its sweet strife,
Fragments of liberation, the essence of life.

Threads of a New Destiny

In colors bright the banners sway,
Laughter rings, it's a joyful day.
We weave our dreams with hearts so bold,
In every thread, a story told.

The dance of joy in twinkling lights,
Together we embrace the nights.
With hands entwined, we spin and twirl,
A vibrant tapestry unfurl.

The moments shared, we hold them tight,
Each heartbeat syncs with pure delight.
In this embrace, our spirits soar,
A tapestry of evermore.

We're threads that shine, so bright, so free,
In unity, we dance with glee.
From every stitch, new hopes arise,
In destiny's web, we claim our skies.

The Unseen Escape

A whisper floats on evening air,
The dance of shadows, light laid bare.
In hidden corners, laughter plays,
While stars ignite the velvet haze.

Through moonlit paths, our spirits glide,
In freedom's arms, we take our stride.
Our hearts collide in joyous swell,
Where unseen whispers weave and dwell.

A gentle breeze, the night invites,
We chase the dreams, on whispered flights.
The world outside fades far away,
In this escape, we bravely sway.

With every step, we find our truth,
In festive echoes, we embrace youth.
The unseen bonds that tie us here,
In joyful presence, we persevere.

Paths of Light

With lanterns lit, the streets come alive,
We gather close, in joy, we thrive.
The laughter spills like summer rain,
Each moment cherished, free from pain.

Underneath the sky, a canvas bright,
We paint our dreams with pure delight.
Footsteps dancing on cobblestone,
In every heart, a spark is sown.

Together we blaze these paths of light,
In every heartbeat, pure delight.
With kindred souls who walk the way,
The festival unfolds in the play.

Imagine sights and sounds that blend,
As every path begins to mend.
In light we trust, through night we roam,
In joy, we find our merry home.

Heartbeats in the Dark

In quiet moments, hearts align,
With every beat, our dreams combine.
The stars emerge, a cosmic dance,
In every glance, the world enchants.

We gather close to share the beats,
In whispered words, our solace greets.
Amidst the shadows, spirits play,
As laughter sparks the night away.

With every heartbeat, joy ignites,
A melody that soars to heights.
In the dark, where shadows spark,
We build our dreams, our vibrant arc.

United in this festive thrill,
Our hearts entwined, they sing and spill.
In nighttime's hush, we forge our song,
With heartbeats strong, we all belong.

After the Night

The stars have shone their light,
As dawn begins to play,
With laughter in the air,
We greet the joyful day.

In colors bright and bold,
The world comes back to life,
With music sweetly told,
As hearts are free from strife.

The warmth of friends around,
Together we will dance,
In every joyful sound,
We find our spirit's chance.

So let the candles glow,
And happiness abound,
For after every night,
A new hope can be found.

Breaching the Limits

Our laughter floats on air,
As fireworks light the night,
We dance without a care,
In dreams that feel so bright.

With every cheer and song,
We break each boundary set,
In unity so strong,
There's no room for regret.

The moments swiftly pass,
Yet memories they weave,
In celebration's grass,
Together we believe.

So raise your glass so high,
To all we've yet to see,
In joy we touch the sky,
With hearts forever free.

Pathways to the Unknown

With lanterns aglow, we stroll,
Through paths where magic lies,
Each step a brand new roll,
Underneath the starry skies.

The whispers of the night,
Invite us to explore,
With every spark of light,
New wonders to adore.

In laughter and delight,
We gather hand in hand,
Embracing every sight,
In this enchanted land.

So let the journey start,
With spirits wild and true,
For every beating heart,
Finds joy in something new.

Light in the Distance

Across the sparkling waves,
A beacon starts to shine,
It calls us in our ways,
A promise so divine.

In echoes of the past,
We chase that flick'ring flame,
In every joy that lasts,
We celebrate our name.

With blissful hearts we run,
Towards that guiding light,
In steps of purest fun,
We dance into the night.

So join this merry throng,
Together we shall be,
Where shadows can't belong,
And joy is all we see.

The Essence of Release

Laughter dances on the breeze,
Joyful hearts share vibrant glee.
Colors swirl in wild embrace,
Moments cherished, time can't erase.

Balloons rise to touch the sky,
Whispers of dreams soar up high.
Each note sung a spirit's call,
Together, we can conquer all.

Candles flicker, spirits ignite,
Hope and love shine warm and bright.
Hands unite in joyful song,
In this place where all belong.

As the night begins to fade,
Memories dance, sweetly laid.
The essence of release, we find,
In laughter shared, our hearts aligned.

A Glimmer in the Gloom

Under shadows, glimmers shine,
Tiny sparks of hope divine.
Gather close, let courage bloom,
Hearts entwined, dispelling gloom.

Candles lit on tables bright,
Warming souls, embracing light.
With each hug, the worries cease,
In this space, we find our peace.

Songs of joy around us soar,
Lifting spirits evermore.
A tapestry of dreams unfolds,
In every heart, a story told.

As the stars begin to gleam,
Hope ignites, a gentle dream.
Together, through the shadows roam,
In love, we've built our home.

The Canvas of Freedom

Brushes dipped in colors bright,
Painting joy, igniting light.
Every stroke, a tale to share,
Freedom whispers in the air.

Music flows like rivers wide,
Join the dance, let spirits glide.
Each heartbeat, a drum in tune,
Underneath the glowing moon.

Glittering stars in velvet skies,
Reflections of our dreams arise.
Together we create the scene,
In this moment, we are free.

Voices rise, a chorus strong,
Unified, we sing along.
The canvas brightens, joy released,
In every heart, a loving feast.

Faces in the Wind

Glistening smiles in the breeze,
Echo laughter through the trees.
Faces bright and spirits high,
Together where our dreams can fly.

Joyful moments weave the tale,
Colorful kites rise and sail.
Children's giggles, pure delight,
Painting joy on canvas bright.

In the rush of joyful play,
Time won't take these days away.
Underneath the sun's warm glow,
Love and kindness truly flow.

As the sunset paints the sky,
Dreams take flight, we learn to fly.
In the wind, our laughter twirls,
Faces radiant, our hearts unfurl.

Breaking the Silence

The drums of joy begin to play,
Voices soar in bright array,
Colors dance across the sky,
Together we will laugh and sigh.

Banners waving, spirits high,
Underneath the sun's soft eye,
Echoes blend, a vibrant mix,
Life unfolds in joyful flicks.

Candles light the evening's glow,
Warmth and love in every flow,
Friends and family all around,
In this moment, bliss is found.

Celebration paints the night,
Hearts ignited, pure delight,
Breaking silence, we unite,
In this dance, all is right.

A Journey Unbound

Pack your dreams, let's hit the road,
With hope and laughter, share the load,
Footsteps echo on the ground,
In the journey, joy is found.

Mountains high and rivers wide,
Every moment, side by side,
The horizon calls our name,
With each mile, we'll stoke the flame.

Stars will guide us through the night,
Chasing visions, pure delight,
Freedom whispers in the breeze,
Together, let's embrace this tease.

No destination, just the ride,
Hearts as compass, souls as guide,
A journey shared, a tale profound,
In every heartbeat, love is found.

Threads of Liberation

A tapestry of dreams unfolds,
Woven threads of tales untold,
Each stitch a moment, bold and bright,
Together we ignite the light.

In every hue, a story lives,
The fabric of our spirit gives,
Voices rise in harmony's song,
United in where we belong.

Freedom dances in the air,
With every heartbeat, we declare,
No more chains, our spirits free,
In this moment, let it be.

Through winding paths and open skies,
We'll paint the world through grateful eyes,
Threads of love, our hands entwined,
In liberation, joy we find.

When the Walls Fall

When the walls that brake us fade,
Joyful hearts, no longer weighed,
Breaking free, a brand-new start,
In this moment, feel the heart.

Laughter echoes through the streets,
Where hope and possibility meets,
Hand in hand, we celebrate,
Together we will elevate.

Colors burst and spirits soar,
Unity we can't ignore,
Fences down, our voices blend,
In a chorus without end.

This is life, a vibrant call,
Together rising, we won't fall,
When the walls come down, we see,
The beauty of our unity.

Boundless Journeys

We gather 'round, the laughter swells,
With tales of hope and magic spells.
The stars align, our spirits soar,
Embracing dreams we can't ignore.

With every step, new paths unfold,
Adventures bright, our hearts behold.
The air is sweet with joy and cheer,
As friendships grow, we draw them near.

In vibrant hues, the world ignites,
With dancing shadows under lights.
Together we create the song,
As time stands still, where we belong.

So raise a glass, let's celebrate,
These moments shared that feel so great.
With open hearts, we find our way,
In boundless journeys, come what may.

Dreams and Dusk

As twilight drapes the sky in gold,
We gather close, our stories told.
The whispers dance on evening air,
While laughter mingles everywhere.

The stars peek out with twinkling eyes,
Reflecting hopes that never die.
Each moment shared a cherished thread,
Of dreams we weave while day has fled.

A tapestry of joy unfolds,
In every smile, a tale of old.
Together we embrace the night,
With hearts aglow, everything feels right.

With every wish upon a star,
We find our peace, no distance far.
In dreams and dusk, we share our glow,
As time flows on, our spirits grow.

The Light Between

In every glance, a spark ignites,
Connecting souls on starry nights.
The laughter flows like rivers true,
In this bright dance, just me and you.

Through shadows deep, we find our way,
With all our fears held at bay.
The light between, it guides our path,
Each moment shared, forever last.

Through whispered dreams, our spirits rise,
As hopes alight in painted skies.
Together here, our hearts align,
In every beat, your hand in mine.

We'll chase the dawn with open hearts,
From dusk to light, a world apart.
In every smile, we'll brightly shine,
Together bound, forever fine.

Unlocked Hearts

With laughter ringing in the air,
We open up, our hearts laid bare.
In joyful moments, love will spark,
As we connect, igniting dark.

The magic flows like vibrant streams,
Where hopes align and shine like dreams.
With every word, a bond we share,
In spaces filled with love and care.

As stars above begin to gleam,
We drift together in a dream.
Unlocked hearts dance through the night,
In harmony, we find our light.

So here we stand, with spirits free,
In every laugh, a symphony.
With open arms, we greet the sun,
Our journey's new, but just begun.

The Light of a Distant Star

Twinkling bright in the velvet night,
Whispers of joy dance in the air.
Laughter erupts, hearts feel light,
Magic weaves through dreams laid bare.

Balloons float high, colors gleam,
Faces aglow, smiles so wide.
Celebration bursts like a dream,
Together we stand, side by side.

Fireworks crackle, stars ignite,
Moments captured, forever ours.
Songs carry forth with pure delight,
Under the spell of radiant stars.

With every cheer, every joyful sound,
A tapestry woven, hearts entwined.
In the glow of love, we are found,
The light of a distant star combined.

Silent Cries in the Night

In shadows deep where whispers dwell,
Dreams encircle like a soft sigh.
A shimmer of hope, like a secret spell,
Dances on wings of the night sky.

A quiet hum of a world unseen,
Gentle murmurs of life's embrace.
Echoes of laughter, a melody keen,
Crafting joy in this sacred space.

Underneath the glittering stars,
Silent cries turn to joyous rejoicing.
Spirits ascend beyond the bars,
Bound by love, with hearts rejoicing.

When dawn breaks, and shadows fade,
The night's magic will still remain.
In every heart, stories parade,
Silent cries turn to joy's refrain.

The Cage and the Key

In a world where dreams can roam,
Cages built of doubt and fear.
Yet hidden somewhere, a heart can home,
The key to freedom, shining clear.

Laughter rings through the heavy air,
Hope ignites with every cheer.
With every step, we shed despair,
Unshackled souls begin to steer.

The night blooms bright with colorful spark,
Joyful echoes fill the lane.
Breaking free from the lingering dark,
Embracing love, escaping pain.

Together we dance, no cage can confine,
With the key of dreams, we take flight.
In this realm where spirits align,
The cage dissolves, bathed in light.

Journey to the Other Side

On this path where wishes tread,
Footsteps light on the golden sand.
With every heartbeat, hope is spread,
A chance to soar, a chance to stand.

Bright lanterns glow, guiding the way,
Through valleys wide and hills so high.
Each moment gathers, a grand array,
Journeying forth, the stars our guide.

We whisper dreams to the moonlit night,
As laughter glimmers like waves in the tide.
Hearts intertwined in the shimmering light,
Together we leap, in joy we ride.

To the other side, where wonders await,
Celebrations echo, spirits alive.
With every heartbeat, we create,
A canvas of love where dreams thrive.

Unfolding Fate

In the air, laughter floats, bright and clear,
Colors swirl, joy draws us near.
The sun shines down on this merry scene,
Hearts are light, as if in a dream.

Banners wave in the gentle breeze,
Time slows down, all worries ease.
Together we dance, under skies so blue,
A tapestry woven with moments new.

From the corners of streets, music calls,
Echoes of festivity fill the halls.
In each twirl and spin, fate intertwines,
Our souls entwined in joyous designs.

The Stretch of Eternity

Beneath the stars, the night aglow,
Candles flicker, casting a warm flow.
Laughter spills like a sweet refrain,
Each moment savored, free from pain.

The moon all smiles, a witness bright,
Embraces the world in silvery light.
With friends around, and spirits high,
We gathered here, hearts flying high.

Stories shared, memories made,
In this circle, love won't fade.
The stretch of time feels like a dance,
In this festival of life, we take a chance.

A Dance with Shadows

In twilight's glow, our shadows play,
Twisting and turning, they sway and sway.
We laugh and sing, chasing the night,
In festive spirits, everything feels right.

The stars above, like diamonds shine,
Illuminating paths, a grand design.
Together we leap, in joy we trust,
With every heartbeat, we create a thrust.

The rhythm pulses, our feet like fire,
Amidst the shadows, we climb higher.
In this moment, we feel so free,
A dance with shadows, just you and me.

Unveiling Hidden Horizons

Beyond the hills, a new dawn breaks,
With every sunrise, a chance that wakes.
Colors burst across the vast expanse,
A festival of dreams, we dare to dance.

Each laugh a promise, each cheer a song,
In unity, where we all belong.
The air is thick with hope and delight,
Together we step into the light.

Hidden horizons, waiting to be found,
In every heartbeat, friendship surrounds.
We celebrate life, our spirits entwined,
In this festive magic, our souls aligned.

The Horizon Calls

Beneath the azure sky so wide,
Laughter dances from side to side.
Joyful spirits rise and fall,
Echoing the horizon's call.

Bright banners wave in gentle breeze,
Whispers carry through the trees.
A melody of dreams unfolds,
As stories of the past are told.

Colors flash and hearts ignite,
Every moment feels so right.
With each cheer, the world aligns,
Gathered here, our spirit shines.

As sunlight fades, the stars appear,
Together we will persevere.
The horizon beckons, shining bright,
In festive joy, we find our light.

Breaking the Silence

In the stillness, laughter breaks,
A sudden joy that laughter makes.
Voices mingle, sweet and clear,
The sound of love is drawing near.

Fireflies dance as night takes flight,
Their glow adds to the warm delight.
Hearts are open, spirits free,
In this festive tapestry.

The quiet quiets, now alive,
As dreams awaken, hopes arrive.
Together under starry skies,
A symphony of life arises.

Each heartbeat echoes, full of cheer,
In this moment, we draw near.
Breaking silence with a song,
In festive unity, we belong.

Emancipation's Song

From shackles cast, the spirit soars,
A vibrant tune that opens doors.
With every note, we rise and sing,
Emancipation's joy we bring.

Colors weave through evening air,
Joyful hearts, we boldly share.
With every step, the past we shed,
In this celebration, fears are fed.

Rhythms thrum with freedom's might,
As we dance beneath the light.
Voices blend in joyous cheer,
In emancipation, we draw near.

Each heartbeat echoes in the night,
Together, we embrace the light.
A song of hope, forever strong,
In festive unity, we belong.

Footsteps in the Open

Through fields of gold, our footsteps tread,
With laughter bright, where dreams are spread.
Each shared moment, a joyful start,
Here in the open, we find our heart.

In the sun's embrace, shadows wane,
Spirits dance in the lively lane.
Freedom's breath fills the fragrant air,
Together, there's no weight to bear.

The world around us sings and sways,
In the festive warmth of sunny days.
With every step, our voices rise,
In unison, under the skies.

Connection thrives in joyous sound,
In open spaces, love is found.
So let us wander, side by side,
In festive cheer, our hearts collide.

The Great Escape

Laughter dances in the air,
Colors twirl like dreams laid bare.
Drums are beating, feet take flight,
Joy ignites the vibrant night.

Stars above in twinkling cheer,
Whispers of adventure near.
Friends unite with hearts ablaze,
Together, lost in festive haze.

Candles flicker, shadows play,
Memories chase the night away.
In this moment, free we sigh,
The world awaits, let's fly high.

With every note and every cheer,
Hope is born, we persevere.
Hand in hand, through joys we skate,
In this rhythm, we escape.

Unshackled Souls

Chains of worry fall away,
Time to laugh, to dance, to sway.
In the glow of friendly light,
We reclaim our endless night.

Voices lift to meet the sky,
In the stars, our dreams will fly.
With each heartbeat, we are bold,
Unshackled souls, our tales unfold.

Moments weave with threads of gold,
Every story shared, retold.
In this garden, spirits bloom,
Joyous echoes fill the room.

Raise a glass to laughter's art,
Celebrate this beating heart.
Together here, we break the mold,
In this magic, we're consoled.

The Call of the Wild

Whispers echo through the trees,
Nature sings upon the breeze.
Hearts are wild, untamed, and free,
Join the call of jubilee.

Wanderlust ignites our souls,
Adventure waits, it gently rolls.
With every step, we chase the light,
In this forest, pure delight.

Campfire crackles, stories thrive,
In this space, we come alive.
Around the flames, our laughter blends,
In this magic, time suspends.

Lift your voice, together loud,
In the wild, we find our crowd.
Dance beneath the moonlit sky,
With open hearts, we soar and fly.

Where Spirits Soar

In the twilight, colors rise,
Echoing through open skies.
Fireworks burst, a grand parade,
Hearts united, fears allayed.

Joyful whispers fill the night,
In this moment, pure delight.
With each hug and shared embrace,
Our spirits soar, a boundless space.

Every note a love-filled song,
Together here, we all belong.
Celebration, sweet and bright,
Carry on till morning's light.

In the laughter, in the cheers,
We create our joyful years.
Hand in hand, through dreams we weave,
In this dance, we truly believe.

A Sea of Stars

In the sky, a dance unfolds,
Twinkling lights like dreams told.
Whispers of joy in the night,
Gathered hearts, so warm and bright.

Laughter echoes, friends unite,
Underneath the glowing light.
Waves of joy, like tides they swell,
A sea of stars, we weave our spell.

Dancing shadows, laughter flows,
In this moment, magic grows.
Every heartbeat, every smile,
Draws us closer, just a while.

Embrace the night, let spirits soar,
In this festivity, we adore.
Together we shine, like constellations,
A sea of stars, our celebrations.

Paint with Light

Brush strokes of laughter fill the air,
Colors twirl in movements rare.
Joyous rhythms, vibrant sounds,
In this canvas, life abounds.

Sparkling eyes, forever gleam,
Every moment, a vivid dream.
Swirls of color in our path,
Create a joy that will never fade.

As we dance through painted skies,
The world is brightened, spirits rise.
With every beat, our passions ignite,
Together we paint, we paint with light.

Festive echoes, hearts so free,
In this creation, just you and me.
A masterpiece of love and cheer,
In every stroke, our bond is clear.

Finding the Exit

Through the maze of joy we roam,
In laughter's grasp, we find a home.
Pathways brightened by our smiles,
A festive spirit spans the miles.

Twists and turns, the music flows,
In every echo, adventure grows.
Following the light, hearts combined,
Together we seek, our path aligned.

Moments fleeting, time's embrace,
With every step, we quicken the pace.
In this maze, there's no regret,
For in the journey, joy is met.

Hands held tight, we face the night,
Finding moments filled with light.
Through the laughter, we discover bliss,
In every exit, a cherished kiss.

Darting Through Dimensions

Waves of laughter, colors blend,
A festive journey without end.
Through dimensions bright, we dart,
Every moment, a beating heart.

Time spirals in a joyful race,
Each dimension, a new embrace.
Spirits high, we leap and glide,
In this dance, we dare not hide.

Euphoria weaves through every thread,
Memories cherished, laughter spread.
Facing worlds where dreams take flight,
Together we shine, a starry night.

Darting through, with hearts so bold,
In every adventure, joy unfolds.
As we journey, let love be our guide,
Through dimensions, forever side by side.

When Dreams Take Flight

In the sky, balloons ascend,
Colors dance, as wishes mend.
Laughter echoes through the night,
Hearts ignite as dreams take flight.

Stars are twinkling, hopes unite,
Candles flicker, warm and bright.
Joyful whispers fill the air,
Magic moments, everywhere.

Children's laughter rings so clear,
Every smile, we hold so dear.
Chasing shadows, feeling free,
In this dream, just you and me.

When the clock strikes midnight's chime,
We'll remember this sweet time.
For in our hearts, the joy will stay,
As we dance the night away.

The Distant Canvas

Brushstrokes billow, colors blend,
On the canvas, tales transcend.
Life's a mural, bold and bright,
Every hue a pure delight.

Voices sing of summer's glow,
Festival spirits start to flow.
In the air, a sweet perfume,
Artists painting joy in bloom.

Children gather, dreams align,
Drawing futures, hearts entwined.
With each splash, the world ignites,
Celebrating our shared sights.

As the sun begins to set,
On this canvas, no regret.
Colors fade but memories stay,
In this moment, we will play.

Longing for Tomorrow

Stars are shining, wishes cast,
Hopeful hearts, we hold steadfast.
Tomorrow beckons, bright and new,
Joyful paths await our view.

In the distance, laughter calls,
Echoes dancing through the halls.
With our friends, we share a dream,
Life's a never-ending theme.

As the world turns with a smile,
We find magic, every mile.
Hand in hand, we chase the sun,
In this journey, we are one.

With each sunset, we find grace,
In every challenge, we embrace.
Longing for what lies ahead,
In love's warmth, we're gently led.

Breaking the Silence

Joy bells ringing, spirits soar,
In the stillness, hearts explore.
Laughter bubbling, breaking free,
In this moment, just you and me.

As the night begins to glow,
Whispers soft like falling snow.
We share secrets, dreams unfold,
Each word precious, worth its gold.

Beneath the stars, we twirl around,
In this silence, love is found.
With each heartbeat, we create,
A symphony that can't wait.

From the quiet, joy will rise,
Painting colors in the skies.
Breaking silence, love, delight,
Eternal magic, pure and bright.

Whispers of the Infinite

Stars sparkle bright in the velvet sky,
Laughter dances like fireflies nearby.
Joyful hearts gather, let spirits soar,
Embracing the magic that we adore.

Songs of the night weave stories untold,
Glimmers of hope in the warmth of the gold.
Celebrate moments, both big and small,
In the glow of togetherness, we stand tall.

Whispers of Freedom

Breezes of light through the branches sway,
Bright banners ripple, in colors they play.
Voices unite in a joyous refrain,
Celebrating life, in sun or in rain.

Candles alight, casting shadows so sweet,
Dancing in circles, our hearts feel the beat.
Boundless horizons call out to our dreams,
In the warmth of the moment, we bask in the gleams.

Shadows of the Unseen

Twinkling lanterns fill the cool midnight,
Echoes of laughter, so pure, so bright.
Murmurs of kindness swirl all around,
In the gentle starlight, our joy is found.

Mysteries linger in whispers of air,
Under the moon, we release every care.
Holding hands tightly, we cherish the bliss,
In the shadows unseen, we find our true kiss.

Through the Unlocked Door

Steps on the path where the wildflowers grow,
Open the door to adventures below.
Colors and laughter to fill up the day,
Together we wander, come join the play.

Feasts of delight spread with love on the way,
Voices and songs echo, come what may.
In this tapestry rich, let our spirits blend,
Through the unlocked door, let the joy never end.

The Uncharted Sky

Beneath the stars, we twirl and spin,
With laughter bright, the night begins.
A canvas vast, where dreams ignite,
We dance in joy, 'neath twinkling light.

Exploring realms where wishes soared,
With hearts ablaze, we moved toward.
The Milky Way, our guiding thread,
In festive moments, hope is spread.

Each shimmer tells a story grand,
Of promies made, and love so planned.
In this embrace, we lose all time,
A celebration, pure and prime.

As dawn breaks forth, we toast to days,
With gleaming eyes, we sing our praise.
For in the sky, our spirits fly,
Together bound, we reach the high.

Dreams of the Open

In fields of gold, we laugh and play,
With summer's scent, we greet the day.
A world unfurls, as hopes take flight,
In every heart, a spark of light.

The breeze whispers tales from afar,
Of journeys made beneath the stars.
We chase the sun, with arms stretched wide,
For every step, it's joy we ride.

A picnic spread, with friends so dear,
With every cheer, we cast out fear.
In vibrant blooms, we find our peace,
In nature's arms, our souls release.

With wines and songs, the night will reign,
As laughter dances, joy unchained.
In dreams so bright, we write our lore,
The open holds, forever more.

The Other Side of Night

When shadows fade, the stars emerge,
In twilight's glow, our spirits surge.
With moonlit paths, we wander free,
Embracing all, as we will be.

The quiet hum of joy ignites,
As friends gather, beneath the lights.
With stories shared, our hearts entwine,
In every laugh, a sip of wine.

We toast to dreams that chase the dawn,
Where all our worries are reborn.
In candle's flicker, secrets swirl,
A magic spell, in every whirl.

As night unfolds, we dance till day,
In rhythmic beats, our souls will sway.
A festive song for every heart,
The other side, a brand new start.

In Search of the Unwritten

With ink and brush, we start anew,
In blank canvases, dreams break through.
In every stroke, our spirits blend,
With colors bright, the night won't end.

We seek the tales yet to unfold,
In whispered dreams, and laughter bold.
A quest for words that sing with pride,
In every heart, the world inside.

Together here, we share the night,
With open hearts, we chase the light.
In every smile, a spark is born,
In stories shared, our hopes adorn.

So raise your glass to paths untold,
With every dream, we break the mold.
The unwritten waits, with arms spread wide,
In life's festivity, we will glide.

The Unbroken Spirit

In the heart of joy, we gather near,
Laughter dances, filled with cheer.
Colors bright in every eye,
We lift our voices to the sky.

Hands entwined, a vibrant chain,
Together we stand, sharing the gain.
With every moment, we ignite,
The fire of hope that shines so bright.

In rhythm of hearts, we sway and sing,
The festive warmth that love can bring.
No shadow casts, no fear to find,
In this embrace, we're intertwined.

Celebrate the bonds we've made,
With every laugh, the past will fade.
The unbroken spirit lives within,
In this festival, let joy begin.

Beyond the Grey

When clouds drift by, and skies turn blue,
A world awakens, refreshed and new.
Songs of hope fill the air,
As we dance away every care.

Banners flutter in gentle breeze,
Whispers of joy among the trees.
Children laughing, spirits soar,
Together we revel, longing for more.

With every beat, our hearts align,
In moments like these, we truly shine.
Beyond all grey, our dreams take flight,
In unity we bask, hearts alight.

So raise a glass, let's toast the night,
To laughter and love, to pure delight.
Together we thrive, come what may,
In this shared moment, beyond the grey.

The Canvas Outside

The canvas outside, a palette bright,
Splash of colors, pure delight.
Nature sings a vibrant tune,
As sunbeam dances with the moon.

Children run on fields of gold,
A story of wonder, waiting to unfold.
The laughter echoes, sweet and clear,
In this painted world, we gather near.

Every flower a brushstroke fair,
With fragrance rich, perfuming the air.
Joy spills over like paint from a jar,
In this masterpiece, we shine like stars.

Let's dance beneath the painted sky,
With every heartbeat, our spirits fly.
The canvas outside, forever so grand,
In this vibrant world, let's take a stand.

Notes of a Forgotten Tune

In the whispers of the night, we share,
Notes of joy float in the air.
A melody missed, now comes alive,
In every heart, the rhythms thrive.

With every chord, we feel the beat,
A symphony that warms our feet.
Together we hum, our voices unite,
In this forgotten tune, pure delight.

Dance with me in the moonlight glow,
Rekindling memories from long ago.
The laughter and song, a timeless embrace,
In every note, we find our place.

Let's weave this night with stories bright,
Creating a tapestry, our hearts take flight.
In the echoes of love, we gently swoon,
Finding joy in this forgotten tune.

The Path Untraveled

Footsteps dance on golden leaves,
Laughter sparkles in the air.
Colors swirl like vibrant dreams,
Joyful hearts free from care.

Twinkling lights and sweet delight,
Gather round, let stories flow.
Each new turn brings fresh delight,
Together, watch the lanterns glow.

Whispers carried on the breeze,
Echoes of a fleeting song.
In this moment, time can freeze,
Here is where we all belong.

With each step, a new surprise,
Every laugh a cherished gift.
In the wonder, hope will rise,
Our spirits soar, our worries lift.

Reflections in the Darkness

Stars above in velvet skies,
Sparkling gems in night's embrace.
Underneath a world of sighs,
We find joy in quiet grace.

Candles flicker, shadows sway,
Hearts entwined in whispered dreams.
Every moment, magic plays,
Binding us with glowing seams.

Echoes of a distant cheer,
Ornaments of laughter bright.
Moments shared, we hold so dear,
In the calm, love shines its light.

Through the veil, our spirits soar,
Together in this sacred space.
In the dark, we learn to roar,
Each reflection, a warm embrace.

Tales of the Unfettered

In the fields where wildflowers bloom,
Freedom calls us, bright and clear.
Chasing dreams that lift the gloom,
Laughter echoes, joy draws near.

Windswept paths and open skies,
Secrets shared beneath the sun.
In our hearts, adventure lies,
Every moment, just begun.

Fires crackle, stories flow,
Dance beneath the starlit night.
With each tale, our spirits grow,
In the warmth, our dreams ignite.

Together, we embrace the call,
Boundless laughter fills the air.
In this world, we stand so tall,
Such is joy, beyond compare.

A World Outside the Window

Raindrops tap on window panes,
Nature's song a joyful tune.
Wild adventures in our veins,
Awake beneath the gentle moon.

Children playing in the street,
Colors dancing, hearts alive.
Every moment, pure and sweet,
In this world, our spirits thrive.

Branches swaying, whispers call,
Flowers bloom in vibrant hues.
In this realm, we have it all,
With open hearts, we can choose.

Through the glass, we see the light,
Every shadow brings a spark.
In the warmth of day and night,
Life unfolds, a joyful arc.

Freedom's Whisper

In the dance of the vibrant night,
Joyful laughter takes its flight.
Colors swirl in a dazzling spree,
Hearts are light, wild, and free.

Music plays, a sweet refrain,
Echoes soft in the gentle rain.
Together we rise, hand in hand,
Unveiling dreams, a festive band.

Glistening stars adorn the sky,
We are alive, let spirits fly.
In every hug, a promise gleams,
United souls, we're part of dreams.

In the wake of the evening's glow,
Love ignites, a warm tableau.
Freedom whispers, soft and clear,
Celebrate life, we're gathered here.

The Cage and the Sky

Inside a cage, thoughts were confined,
Yet the heart sought all that's divine.
With every beat, a longing grew,
To touch the sky, a dream to pursue.

Feathers of hope began to sprout,
Against the odds, we scream and shout.
Together we break the heavy chain,
As laughter spills through joy and pain.

Under the sun, with arms out wide,
The horizon's promise, our joyful guide.
With every step, the world feels bright,
In the embrace of shimmering light.

The cage behind, the sky ahead,
With every move, we're gently led.
Through fields of gold, our spirits soar,
In unity, we seek for more.

Echoes of the Unseen

Whispers dance on the evening breeze,
Softly carrying moments with ease.
In every shimmer, a story spins,
Of laughter shared and joyful wins.

The unseen magic, vibrant and bold,
In every heart, warmth to hold.
As colors burst and spirits collide,
In harmony, we find our stride.

Cascades of joy, like stars that gleam,
We weave together, a radiant team.
With each heartbeat, the promise stays,
In echoes of love, we find our ways.

The night unfolds, alive and bright,
In every glimmer, pure delight.
Together we soar, like birds in flight,
In endless joy, our hearts ignite.

Chains Left Behind

In shadows past, we shed our fears,
With every tear, we dry our cheers.
Chains that bound now fall away,
In freedom's light, we choose to play.

With open hearts, we gather round,
Celebrating the love we've found.
In unity, our voices rise,
Together we break through the skies.

The future calls, bright and new,
Woven dreams in every hue.
Hands entwined, we leap and glide,
With joyous hearts, we turn the tide.

Chains left behind, we now embrace,
A tapestry of hope and grace.
In every smile, a world reborn,
In festive spirit, we greet the morn.

Unwritten Journeys

In the glow of lantern light, we dance,
Every laugh a step, each smile a chance.
Colors swirl like dreams in flight,
Together we weave a tapestry bright.

Under starlit skies, tales unfold,
Adventures whispered, brave and bold.
Hearts entwined, we're never apart,
Every journey begins with a spark.

With every moment, stories ignite,
In the warmth of friendship, all feels right.
Paths unknown, but hope lights the way,
In this festive glow, come what may.

Let's raise a glass to roads not taken,
In laughter and joy, our fears awaken.
For each unwritten tale still to be,
The joy of travel is sweet and free.

Chasing the Horizon

Golden rays paint the morning sky,
With every step, our spirits fly.
We chase the sun, that fiery sphere,
In the distance, dreams appear.

Laughter rings through fields of gold,
Stories shared, memories bold.
With loved ones close, we feel the thrill,
In this vibrant world, our hearts are filled.

Each moment passed, a treasure found,
Earth beneath us, joy's resound.
Chasing horizons, the day is bright,
Together we soar, hearts taking flight.

With every sunset, colors blend,
In this fleeting light, our spirits mend.
The journey continues, our hearts alive,
In the festival of life, we thrive.

Hopes Gleaned from Struggle

From shadows rise the tales we tell,
In every challenge, we find our spell.
Hands once heavy, now lift the prize,
Through trials faced, our courage flies.

In the darkest night, a glimmer shines,
Each tear we shed, a path aligns.
With every hardship, strength we gain,
Through the storms, we dance in rain.

We gather dreams like stars in hands,
In unity, our hope expands.
Through laughter, tears, and bonds so tight,
We ignite the spark, embrace the light.

A festive spirit in struggles' embrace,
Together we find our destined place.
With hearts aglow, we rise as one,
In the glow of triumph, we've just begun.

When Silence Speaks Loudly

In the hush of dusk, we breathe it in,
Silence wrapped in the warmth of kin.
Every glance a story shared,
In gentle moments, hearts are bared.

Beneath the stars, unspoken words,
Feelings soar like silent birds.
Each heartbeat echoes through the air,
In tranquil peace, an unbreakable care.

With laughter bubbling beneath the still,
In every quiet moment, we feel the thrill.
The calm surrounds, a cherished cloak,
Amongst the stillness, true bonds evoke.

When silence falls, it speaks so clear,
In the company of those we hold dear.
A festive spirit, in this sacred space,
Where words are few, love finds its place.